Hidden Gems

PATRICIA "PJ" JONES
&
DEBRA D JONES

Copyright © 2017 Debra D Jones LLC

All rights reserved. This book or any portion thereof may not be reproduced or used in any manner whatsoever without the express written permission of the publisher except for the use of brief quotations in a book review.

All Scripture references are from the NIV unless otherwise noted and are from the public domain.

Printed in the United States of America.

First Printing, 2017

ISBN: 978-0-9975563-2-2

This book is dedicated to the memory of our beloved Mama - Mildred H. Jones-Lloyd and Step Dad - Eddie Lloyd.

It is also to honor the memory of Maxine Dixon, a precious gem whose shine could not be hidden.

SPECIAL THANKS

We extend thanks to our beautiful families—PJ's daughter, Sonya and son, Brandon and Debra's husband Bill and son, Mike for supporting our endeavors.

CONTENTS

Introduction	1

Part I: Hidden Gems—The Book

Discovery	3
Damaged Goods	9
Separation	13
Clean Hearts	17
Diamonds & Pearls	21
CZ—An Interlude by Alice M. Baker	29

Part II: Hidden Gems Exposed—The Workbook	31

Rediscovering You	35
I'm Good	41
Isolation for Elevation	49
The Master Plan	57
Ready for My Close-Up	63
The Authors Speak	71
Patricia 'PJ' Jones	
Debra D Jones	

Acknowledgments	75
About The Authors	78

Introduction

When I hear the words 'hidden gem' in a sentence, it causes my ears to perk up! I begin to listen intently in expectation of what is coming next. I anxiously await additional details that will lead me to a unique shopping spot, a vacation location in a serene area filled with beauty; perhaps even a restaurant few have experienced with magnificent food.

The idea of a hidden gem evokes a delightful image for me. There is, however, one nagging detail that I usually consider: why is something regarded as a gem hidden in the first place? Is it like some of the beauty that I have passed many times while driving and only notice when I get an opportunity to be a passenger traveling the same road? Are those that are not seeing it missing it because they are focused on other things that demand their attention? Is it purposely placed so that others have to search for it much like one of my favorite childhood games of hide and seek?

There are many answers to my questions and issues you may have as well. With those answers come this obvious truth: things of value, worth, and beauty are often easily hidden in plain sight. Explore the pages of this book and workbook, as valuable items are uncovered; along with eye-opening events that

INTRODUCTION

occurred during a routine shopping trip as hidden gems are exposed!

Things of value, worth, and beauty are often easily hidden in plain sight.

Discovery

What if I told you that I made an amazing discovery without looking for it? There is something that is very exciting about having a eureka experience which is not even remotely the expedition you thought you were on. Well, walk with me as I share what I experienced.

Here's the thing, I was looking for something, just not what I eventually found to be most valuable. Let me explain. I went to a local home décor store one evening. I was looking for a particular item and realized I had struck gold! There was a 90% off Clearance Extravaganza in progress. As a real bargain hunter, this was one of those rare finds that are the thing that dreams are made of and get the adrenaline flowing. I purchased some items and returned the next two days to pick up additional items which I had mentally marked for pick up on my future visits.

To my dismay, on the third day, I found that the nicer things were gone, picked over or broken. Out of disappointment, I started looking around the store in hopes of finding something/anything to make the trip worthwhile. When I calculated my time as well as money spent on gas, it made perfect sense to find something else to spend money on, to justify the trip. I saw no need in wasting a good shopping excursion.

Discovery

I began to walk around the store and right about the time that I was ready to concede to finding nothing; I noticed a beat up cardboard box with some shiny items on the floor. I stooped down to get a better view of the partially hidden box underneath a weathered wooden table. The way it was situated, it was easy to miss. It could've been easy to overlook, as there was not anything distinctive about the box. It was brown, cardboard and a bit worn. Honestly, one may have even mistaken it for trash. It was the shininess that peered over the edge that caught my eye. I stooped down and pulled the box out and realized the shiny items were what looked like gems tightly intermixed with mylar, shredded paper and what appeared to be miscellaneous junk.

I decided, along with encouragement from my knees to pick the box up and place it on the table at a level that would be more comfortable and allow me easier access to its contents. Thoroughly engrossed in searching and untangling the contents of my box, I looked up for a moment and noticed that some of the other shoppers appeared to be skillfully working their way closer to my table to get a better look at my box. Some of them seemed to be pretending not to notice the box or me as they walked closer, touching items on a nearby counter while using their peripheral vision, but I know that game. I felt they were anxiously waiting to see if I would abandon my box and move on so that they could peek inside.

I decided that it was time to move my box and gems to a more secure area out of the watchful eye of the majority of the shoppers. After grabbing a basket, I walked to the rear of the store until I finally came to a section far removed from the general population. I sat down on a bench, removed my box from the basket and continued to untangle my beautiful finds while separating them in a bowl.

The process was slow and tedious, and some of the gems were more complicated to sort out of the pile than others. After sorting through some of the items in the box, I was astonished to have wiggled so much more free than I expected. At this point, I realized that I had spent lots of time there and needed to leave the store and head home. However, I did not wish to run the risk of leaving my box only to return to find it was gone much like the items which I missed out on from my previous visits to the store. It was at this point that I realized if I was to be more focused on the task of untangling and uncovering more gems, I needed a strategy that would gain me more time.

It is fascinating to have a eureka experience unrelated to the expedition you thought you were on

Damaged Goods

I had a light bulb moment! I placed the box and the bowl that I was using to separate the gems back into my basket. I hurried through the store in search of a manager. I decided I would attempt to negotiate a price for the unmarked box and everything in it combined.

My search resulted in two managers consulting each other to set a price. As I stood and waited for their decision, I had already assessed the contents of my basket. The number of gems in the small bowl that I had sat inside the battered box was worth more than the price that I heard the managers quoting. The memory of the lovely items that I missed out on earlier during the week faded quickly. I was very pleased as I thought about how I had barely scratched the surface in freeing some of the gems, not to mention that I had successfully negotiated what I felt was less than 10% of the discounted price for items viewed by others as worthless. The cashier was instructed to sell these items to me as 'Damaged Goods'!

I left the store confident that the price I paid for the box of gems was far less than it was worth. It had become evident to me that they had hidden value. There was no doubt that I had come out the winner in this negotiation. Discovering my shiny gems in a box served as a life lesson for me, and I see parallels to what God can show us. The discovery process of who we are is different for each of us. Some are unable to see beyond what has them entangled such as broken trust, pride, low and no self-esteem, bitterness, resentment, pain, drugs, mental, emotional and physical abuse or whatever else the world has offered. To the natural eye, these entanglements tend to overshadow the beauty that lies within. The Lord, however, wants us to know that we are indeed beautiful the way He created us. He also has a way of rescuing us from what looks like a hopeless situation. Just as the box appeared destined for the trash, some people may look worthless, or all used up. However, God knows our value, and He always has plans for us.

*God has a way of rescuing us from what
may look like a hopeless situation.*

Separation

I exited the store with my box with great excitement. I placed the box in the trunk of my car and headed home. I planned to retrieve the box from the trunk once my husband left for work and begin the task of freeing more of my gems.

Now, let me be very transparent – I had no intention of walking through the front door of our home with a beat up cardboard box full of unrecognizable beauty. I know my husband well enough to know the gems would have to be cleaned up before showing them to him or he might see them as junk.

Not long after my husband pulled out of the driveway, I retrieved my box from the trunk and carried it into the living room. I allowed the entire contents of the box to spill onto the carpet. I sat on the floor and marveled at what I saw before me.

I was stunned at the red, blue, green, purple, white and a few gold gems that lay shining brightly on my floor. Along with my incredible discovery was the reality that it would take some work to untangle them completely. The work would involve removing them from the miscellaneous paper, shredded mylar,

Separation

garland, and I realized there were even some Mardi Gras beads. I initially felt there were a lot of gems, but I had no idea how deeply hidden some of them were until I got further into the process of freeing them.

To avoid the risk of damaging the gems as I untangled them from their mess, I decided to start cutting anything off that was attached to them. Most of them were in mint condition, but some had nicks and smudges. Overall the majority of the gems were in excellent condition.

Due to the volume of these beautiful jewels, it was necessary for me to separate, organize and categorize them to make identification and cleaning easier. Once they were separated, I had piles of red, green, purple, white and gold. There was also a group that included those that were broken or nicked. Of all the gems I had, there were none that I felt should be thrown out because the sheer beauty of them would outshine any flaws.

I had no idea how deeply some of the gems were hidden beneath junk.

Clean Hearts

The jewels discovered on the floor in a beat up cardboard box were now free from the messy state they were found. The entire box of gems was untangled, separated, and categorized, and a general cleaning performed. This process removed the surface dirt and residue. So many beautiful colors, shapes and sizes of gems lay before me. My personal favorite was the heart shaped ones. I began to admire all of them again and realized the gems were gleaming and beautiful, but whenever the light hit some of them in just the right way, you could see small smudges and fingerprints from them being handled. I retrieved a soft white cloth and began to buff them lightly so they would shine. Once this task was complete, I could look at them, see the brilliance they radiated and say, "Now, they are flawless gems!"

As I shared in the beginning, I initially stopped by a home décor store looking for what I wanted and found more than I expected. I needed to see and experience this process to gain insight into what God wanted me to know.

I had great excitement when I discovered the gems. It was in part because of my love for bargains, but also because I am blessed with creative ability to see the potential of things being used in many different ways. The gems I discovered – they were being sold as Christmas ornaments! I have used them as such, but also see more applications for their future including beautiful jewelry and accessories.

The jewels discovered on the floor in a beat up cardboard box were now free from the messy state they were found.

Diamonds & Pearls

Diamonds and Pearls. There was a song by this title performed by a singer known worldwide simply as The Artist. In addition to being a singer with a wide vocal range, he was also a songwriter, producer and accomplished musician. Whether you subscribe to the genre of music he performed or not, he was considered an artistic genius whose work has been released in the earth and influences the lives of many.

Some of you reading this book are gifted and multi-talented as well. Others may see how valuable you are, but you are unable to see or conceive the idea that you may indeed be a genius in your respective area. The ideas that you've executed, the way you can do things effortlessly that many people struggle with and have great difficulty performing, come naturally for you. When you are gifted in an area, it may be difficult to think that other people cannot do the same thing with the ease that you perform so well. Everyone has gifts, and they do not need to be compared to one another to determine their value. They are unique and should be used to the greatest purpose that God has intended. Sometimes the issue with seeing the genius of you could very well be your perception of you! Are you one of the best cooks, writers, singers, songwriters, waitresses, tailors, visionaries, encouragers, speakers, entertainers or teachers to name a few? If you take time to think about it, I bet your answer is Yes!

Look at yourself today through fresh eyes and examine the apparent uniqueness and genius of who you are.

In the world of a gemologist, gems are classified as precious and semi precious. Diamonds and pearls are two examples of gems. When I looked at how a determination is made to value these stones, I saw characteristics that I believe help illustrate determining value in other areas.

The diamond is considered one of the most valuable gems in the world. When the monetary value of a diamond is determined, the industry standard has agreed that four different areas of the gem should be taken into consideration. This rating system known as the 4 C's assesses the four areas of color, clarity, cut, and carat. Let's get some insight by exploring the diamond's defining characteristics.

Color - in this instance when we refer to color, it is the absence of color that is being appraised. It is considered more valuable when its hue is pure, like water.

Clarity - the heat and pressure of forming a diamond can result in a variety of internal characteristics called inclusions and external imperfections called blemishes. If the inclusion or blemish is unable to be detected at 10x magnification, it is considered flawless.

Cut - diamonds are known for their ability to sparkle and transmit light. When you think of the cut, you might believe that it refers to the shape, but the cut is the most complex and technically challenging of all the 4 c's. It requires a skillful artisan to be able to cut it in just the right way so that the facets of the diamond's brightness, fire and sparkle are released.

Carat Weight – although many may be in particular concerned with the size, the weight is what is measured when determining its' carat. The weight is not the sole determining factor of a diamond's valuation. A smaller carat that has been more skillfully cut by an artisan can be of greater value than a large stone unskillfully cut that does not release the full extent of its brilliance.

Now, let's consider the pearl. It is the only stone of precious or semi-precious nature that forms inside a living organism. An oyster with its hinged shell houses the pearl. The type of oyster that produces pearls lives deep within the ocean in one spot its entire life. When a foreign substance like sand threatens it, it creates a smooth layer to cover it. It places layer after layer over the irritant that enters it until a beautiful pearl is produced.

After looking at the information related to diamonds and pearls, I cannot look at another person without considering how valuable they are to God, our Master Craftsman and each other. Even with our blemishes I now know that we can be regarded as flawless, brilliant, cut to perfection and weighty. I also realize that there was a purpose for being in a deep place, having irritant upon irritant put on us while we remained in the same spot until being released for such a time as this. The mystery of the hidden gem is now exposed!

*Even with our blemishes I now know
that we can be regarded as flawless,
brilliant, cut to perfection and weighty.*

CZ — An Interlude

The Introduction of *Hidden Gems* steered us into; Discovery, Damaged Goods, Separation, Clean Hearts, and Diamonds & Pearls. So the question becomes, where are your gems? Are your gems in your CZ's? WOW! Are you serious? After reading about diamonds and pearls, why would there be a question if my gems are in my CZ's? They too are exquisitely cut. However, it is an imitation that has the appearance of a diamond and can never have the form of the elegant pearl. Furthermore, it is without the essential quality, ingredients, and the cost of a diamond.

But, let me come clean. Since we are talking about gems, I know you thought I was referring to cubic zirconia. Not so! Are you ready for this? CZ is "Comfort Zone." What is holding you hostage to the point that you have become complacent? Is it fear? Maybe you feel you are not good enough or smart enough? Are you intimidated by others? Oh, I know, you do not want to fail, or you are afraid to go to the next level because of the unknown. From my own personal experience(s), I have encountered those very same issues. It wasn't until discovery and embracing the gems God deposited in me—I took the leap of faith out of my comfort zone into the place of "no more excuses!" I know who I am and Whose I am. I am not trying to be nor become a carbon copy of anyone else. God never designed me to 'do it' like another. I am unique because that is the way He created me - in His image. We were all fearfully and wonderfully made - created with gems. Therefore, I no longer walk in identity crisis mode. The more I walk in my uniqueness, the more I am loving it. My new comfort zone has become my comfort zone. Old things have passed away and behold all things have become new. (2 Corinthians 5:17) So I challenge you to discover your hidden gems, thank God for them, and move towards your new journey. His Word says He will do a new thing in you. (Isaiah 43:19)

My prayer is that you have been blessed by Part I of Hidden Gems. Hopefully, as you cross the threshold and transition into Part II, "The Workbook" you will begin to see from God's perspective and gain tools to enhance your walk with Him.

The Workbook is stimulating, challenging, and it will bless you immensely. As you venture into it, reflect on, what precious or semiprecious stone(s) are you sitting on that is just waiting to be cut, polished or even engraved? Embrace the diamonds and pearls on the inside of you. Allow Part II to take you to another dimension in Him. Be prayerful and meditate on it. Don't rush! Take your time and allow the Holy Spirit to speak to you. With open hearts and minds, receive what God has specifically carved out just for you. You may have to dig deep to find your hidden treasure, but, I promise it will be well worth it.

My Gems Are No Longer Hidden! They Are Gainfully Employed in My New CZ!

—Alice M. Baker

PART II
HIDDEN GEMS - EXPOSED
THE WORKBOOK

Now that we have exposed the mystery of the hidden gems, the following workbook is designed to allow us to take a closer look at ourselves and gain revelation and insight through Bible Scriptures.

PART II
HIDDEN EMPLOYMENT IN THE WORKPLACE

Introduction to Part II — The Workbook

The first section of this book has served as the backstory of how God revealed the story of Hidden Gems through a shopping adventure. It's nice to hear stories and see how God reveals Himself to others.

This workbook section pushes us a bit further as it requires more than casual observation, it requires participation. If we are to understand who God has intended us to be, why not look in His Word, the Holy Bible to see what His intention is concerning us?

The next chapters challenge us to rediscover who we are and to be honest with ourselves and others when things are not ok. This section will assist us in understanding the purpose of being isolated for a period and help us to become prepared and transparent for close-up inspection. We also look at the Master Plan concerning each of us.

In the following chapters, use the workbook to answer questions about yourself, study, meditate on bible scriptures, and record your observations, insight, and revelation as you – another Hidden Gem is Exposed!

Rediscovering You

Whenever someone tells me that I've changed, I excitedly say "Thank you for noticing!" It is because I realize as long as I am growing, there will be change. When we recognize the power of God and His ability to not only change our circumstances but change us, we can be encouraged.

We have the opportunity to look at where we came from, how God has always viewed us, and how we can view ourselves in this time of rediscovery.

Hidden Gems

Review and respond to the questions below. Meditate on the bible scriptures and journal your thoughts.

1. Where were you when you became aware that God was available to deliver you to a new life?

_____
_____
_____

2. What do you think about who you are and where you are in your life now?

_____
_____
_____

3. Have you taken time to look at yourself in the mirror lately? (Yes/No)
If yes, what do you see in yourself?

_____
_____
_____

If No, Explain

_____
_____
_____

3. What do you think God sees when he looks at you?

_____
_____
_____

Rediscovering You
Bible Scriptures
Study and Meditation

Psalm 40:2 NIV—*He brought me up also out of an horrible pit, out of the miry clay, and set my feet upon a rock, and established my goings.*

Proverbs 31:10 NIV—*Who can find a virtuous and capable wife? She is more precious than rubies.*

Psalm 139:14 NIV—*I praise you because I am fearfully and wonderfully made; your works are wonderful, I know that full well.*

Jeremiah 29:11 NIV—*For I know the plans I have for you," declares the Lord, "plans to prosper you and not to harm you, plans to give you hope and a future.*

Hidden Gems

Rediscovering You

Hidden Gems

I'm Good

"I'm good!" How many of us have responded this way when someone asked us how we were doing when we were far from good? Sometimes it is easier to say that than examine ourselves and be honest with ourselves and others.

"I'm good!" can be a great affirmation that we speak over our lives; however it is important to acknowledge when we have been hurt, offended, damaged or are experiencing lack in resources or health. The purpose of this is not to relive an offending event or expose a private matter; rather it is to acknowledge it and give it over to God because He has already paid the price for any damage done to us and is well able to provide resources and healing for us as well. When He chooses to use others to help, we want to recognize and be open to how He uses people to help one another.

God was so impressed with who He created us to be that He paid full price for us with His life! Now when we say "I'm Good!" it should be a declaration of God's willingness and ability to redeem, heal, transform and provide for us.

Review and respond to the questions below. Meditate on the bible scriptures and journal your thoughts.

1. Do you always answer **TRUTHFULLY** when someone asks how you are doing/feeling? (Yes/No)
If No, Why?

_____
_____
_____

2. *On a scale of 1-10, how do you rate your* **CONFIDENCE** *in expressing your uniqueness with others? (personality, talent, abilities and vulnerabilities)*

(i.e., 1=not confident; 4=somewhat confident; 7=confident; 10= exceptionally confident)

      1 2 3 4 5 6 7 8 9 10

3. *Have you ever had someone 'help' you and not receive the result you desired? (Yes/No)*

If yes, how did you respond?

_____
_____
_____

4. *Do you believe this has influenced your willingness to ask for and/or accept help? (Yes/No)*

If Yes – in what way(s)?

_____
_____
_____

5. *Have you ever had someone 'help' you and not receive the result you desired? (Yes/No)*

If yes, how did you respond?
_____
_____
_____

6. *List three ways to respond when someone says they want to help you:*

    1. _____
    2. _____
    3. _____

Everyone needs help at some point. God wants us to depend on Him and be helpful to each other as well as ask for and accept help when necessary. Here are some things to keep in mind:

    a. *Be clear about what you need help with if you know. There may be times that you have become overwhelmed and someone else may need to make suggestions for the help they can provide.*

    b. *When someone helps you, accept the help in the manner they can render. i.e., If you need help with a resource and they are only able to help with a portion of the resource, be gracious to receive what they can offer.*

    c. *If you are concerned about exposing a private matter, only share what you are comfortable sharing.*

I'M GOOD

> d. Always say "Thank You" to God and others that provide help.

If you are the person that assists others and renders help, be sure that you are in a position to help without becoming overwhelmed, stressed and unable to replenish your time and/ or resources. Now – when you say "I'm Good," be certain it is the truth. If it is not, be as open as necessary with those that can help. Do not be afraid to ask for help when necessary; nor offended when they are unable or unwilling to comply.

Hidden Gems

Bible Scriptures Study and Meditation

Proverbs 18:21 NIV—*The tongue has the power of life and death, and those who love it will eat its fruit.*

Exodus 23:5 NIV—*If you see the donkey of someone who hates you fallen down under its load, do not leave it there; be sure you help them with it.*

Psalm 24:1 NIV—*The earth is the Lord's, and everything in it, the world, and all who live in it*

Hebrews 13:5b NIV—*Never will I leave you; never will I forsake you.*

1 Timothy 2:6a NLT—*He gave his life to purchase freedom for everyone.*

Psalm 121:2 NIV—*My help comes from the Lord, the Maker of heaven and earth.*

Hidden Gems

I'm Good

Hidden Gems

Isolation for Elevation

I have a friend who loves to be around people. She is very creative, capable and diligent but if a project needs to be completed, it likely would not be her first choice to work in solitude. There are others who love people, but their personality type is comfortable and even preferable to working alone in solitude. Although these two personality types are different – one that prefers to be in the presence of others, the other that prefers time alone, neither of these is superior to the other. The one that prefers the company of others may be an extrovert; the one that relishes solitude, an introvert. Introverts generally will need to recharge after spending time with others by spending time alone. Extroverts, on the other hand, recharge and are stimulated when they are in the company of others. Whether an introvert or extrovert, everyone was designed to interact with other people at some time. During these periods of interaction, we may be encouraged by one another, learn and even experience great joy and comfort.

With all this being said, it is difficult to embrace the reality that there may be times that we are placed in a position to spend time alone. Whether we like it or not, there may be times that God wants to isolate us to spend time with us. Alone. This doesn't mean that there is no interaction with others; it could indicate that those times are limited, less stimulating and perhaps even similar to having a peripheral view. You could be in a crowded room where a conversation is happening all around, and you may even try to engage in conversation with others only to feel like your comments are not being heard. There could be times that you would've been the person who is always the first invited to events, asked out for lunch or whose opinion is often solicited; but then those invitations either begin to trickle in or they dry up altogether. If this becomes your situation, it would be a great time to ask God if you are in a state of isolation. If His answer is yes, it will benefit you to get all God has destined for you in your time of isolation.

When God places us in a state of isolation, away from the general population, the noise, the germs that are floating around, the negative behaviors and conversations of others; it is generally for our protection, correction, and redirection.

Isolation for Elevation

Review and respond to the questions below. Meditate on the bible scriptures and journal your thoughts.

1. Do you consider yourself an extrovert, introvert or a combination of the two?
   (circle one)
   a. Extrovert - a person who is social and outgoing
   b. Introvert - a person who is enjoys spending time alone
   c. Ambivert - a person that has both extrovert and introvert characteristics

2. If you have time available, how do you generally use it? (circle all that apply)
   a. Call a friend to catch up
   b. Watch a movie
   c. Pray, read or listen to music that is God-centered (devotional time)
   d. Something else
      (list here)_____

3. If you do not currently have time scheduled each day to devote exclusively to God, here are some suggestions:
   a. Set your alarm clock 15 minutes early
   b. Find a place alone if you can
   c. Have your bible, a notebook and something to write with
   d. Have worship music available (earphones also if you don't want to disturb other members of your household)
   e. Pray for at least 5 minutes without asking God for anything other than the ability to hear from Him clearly and thanking Him
   f. Spend the next 5 minutes reading bible

scriptures

    g. *Use at least 2 of the final 5 minutes to practice being quiet and listening for God's voice. Use the final few minutes to record any revelation God has given you through your time in prayer, reading the Word or during your quiet time.*

Try increasing the amount of time you spend from 15 minutes to as much time as you can with God. I believe you will find that the more time you spend in God's Word and prayer, clarity will manifest that shows you who you are and where you are in relationship to what the bible says – the beauty of who you are as well as the flaws that should and can be corrected.

This process will be like looking in a mirror and realizing that the reflection staring back is you. If you don't like what you see, ask God to show you how to correct your image, so you reflect the true beauty within that He created. When that beauty is reignited and radiates within, it will show up on the outside and propel you in ways you likely did not imagine!

Hidden Gems
Bible Scriptures
Study and Meditation

Psalm 102:7 NIV—*I lie awake; I have become like a bird alone on a roof.*

2 Corinthians 6:17 NIV—*Therefore, "Come out from them and be separate, says the Lord. Touch no unclean thing, and I will receive you."*

Mark 1:12-13 NIV—*At once the Spirit sent him out into the wilderness, and he was in the wilderness forty days, being tempted by Satan. He was with the wild animals, and angels attended him.*

Psalm 51:10 NIV—*Create in me a pure heart, O God, and renew a steadfast spirit within me.*

Hidden Gems

Isolation for Elevation

Hidden Gems

The Master Plan

If you were interested in building your dream home, had unlimited financial resources and wanted to contract someone to design and build that dream home, who would you hire? An apprentice (a person who works for and under someone else to learn a trade) or a master builder (the person that the apprentice is working for and studying under)? Obviously, this is a rhetorical question—you would hire the master builder! The one that is an expert and will be able to bring your dream to fruition at a level that far exceeds the work of others.

Any great builder has created a design with his Master Plan in mind. God is the ultimate Master Builder, and He has a perfect Master Plan revealed through His infallible Word, The Holy Bible.

God in His infinite wisdom created you and defined your role in His Master Plan.

Let's look at what He is revealing to us in the following bible scriptures. Be sure to journal any thoughts or insights He gives you.

Review and respond to the questions below. Meditate on the bible scriptures and journal your thoughts.

1. Have you operated as an apprentice or a master builder in your life? (Apprentice/Master Builder)

   a. What do you think the relationship of an apprentice and master builder should look like?

   _____
   _____
   _____

   b. How can an apprentice benefit under the direction and training of a master builder?

   _____
   _____
   _____

2. If you've ever operated as your own master builder, what do you think caused you to do so? (i.e. no direction from others, the need to be in control, etc)

   a. List causes here:

   _____
   _____
   _____

   b. List any mishaps that could've been prevented if you were not responsible for your own design and build?

   _____
   _____
   _____

Bible Scriptures
Study and Meditation

Proverbs 19:21 NIV *- Many are the plans in a person's heart, but it is the Lord's purpose that prevails.*

Jeremiah 29:11 NIV *- For I know the plans I have for you," declares the Lord, "plans to prosper you and not to harm you, plans to give you hope and a future.*

Ecclesiastes 3:1 NIV - *There is a time for everything, and a season for every activity under the heavens*

Daniel 2:21 NIV *- He changes times and seasons; he deposes kings and raises up others. He gives wisdom to the wise and knowledge to the discerning.*

Deuteronomy 28:12 NIV *- The Lord will open the heavens, the storehouse of his bounty, to send rain on your land in season and to bless all the work of your hands. You will lend to many nations but will borrow from none.*

Hidden Gems

The Master Plan

Hidden Gems

Ready for My Close-up

The time that we live in is technologically advanced and has given us access to information through media, advertising and the like. Reality TV promises to give us a glimpse into the glamorous lives of others; their picture-perfect families, spotless homes, beautiful hair, faces, and clothes. What we don't see is what goes on behind the scenes, we don't see the artists that are erasing blemishes with makeup, the hair stylist that is there to make sure every hair is in place, the crew that makes certain each pillow is correctly placed on the sofa, that there are no unclean dishes in the sink.

We also don't seem to realize that whatever is not perfect can easily be edited out of the final show before it is revealed. If we are not careful, we may be drawn to the glamorization that we see and not realize that reality TV is scripted. We may even be guilty of imagining and wishing our lives mirrored what we perceive as perfect.

God did an interesting thing when He created each of us: He didn't bother to create a mold and make each of us exactly alike, He took time to make us in His image with unique characteristics. We were created intentionally and with great precision and in perfection. We are fearfully and wonderfully made.

This is our reality – God created us to be perfect. Sin in our lives is the variable that pollutes what God made perfect. However, God provides a solution for sin. The life and blood of His only Son, Jesus The Christ!

He can clean us up, erase blemishes, change the very nature, proclivities and look of who we were to the look that is revealed in its perfect state once again. The scripted and edited version of us is when we have accepted the gift of Jesus Christ.

If you have not accepted Him as your personal Lord and Savior, now is as good a time as any to pray based on the summarization of what Romans 10:8-10 says - confess with your mouth and believe in your heart that Jesus died and was raised from the dead and you shall be saved! Pray this prayer "Lord, I make the confession that Jesus died for me and was raised from the dead. I believe this in my heart. I receive my gift of salvation and accept Jesus as my Lord and Savior. In Jesus Name. Amen."

Now – take another look at yourself as you meditate on the bible scriptures and journal your thoughts.

Ready for My Close-up
Bible Scriptures
Study and Meditation

Proverbs 31:10b NIV - *She is worth far more than rubies.*

Proverbs 31:29 NIV - *Many women do noble things, but you surpass them all.*

Isaiah 60:1 NIV - *Arise, shine, for your light has come, and the glory of the Lord rises upon you.*

Matthew 5:16 NIV - *In the same way, let your light shine before others, that they may see your good deeds and glorify your Father in heaven.*

Hidden Gems

Ready for My Close-up

Hidden Gems

Thank you for allowing us to share *Hidden Gems* with you. We hope you have been inspired, encouraged, provoked and enlightened. We desire that you will use this book and workbook as a reminder of how valuable you are to God and others.

The Authors Speak

From Patricia

I have always had a passion for writing. As a teenager, I would spend hours sitting on the floor imagining, dreaming, and writing short stories. This passion for writing led me to take several college writing courses in pursuit of a writing career, however, my dream was deferred when I made a split-second decision to follow a "safer" route and work full-time.

Many years later, my youngest sister, Debra, shared some thoughts that God had spoke to her during a shopping experience. I told her that the experience that she shared sounded like a book and we began to work on a writing project which later became Hidden Gems.

My sister later gave me an online writing course as a birthday gift. She also consistently encouraged me to write, saying things like "PJ, you need to start writing." Working on this book and participating in the online class revived my interest in writing and helped me realize that my sister Debra feels that I am a "Hidden Gem".

To those of you who have read this book, I hope that it encourages you to find the *"Hidden Gem"* in yourself and others.

Connect with Patricia 'PJ' Jones
Facebook @patriciaaJones
Periscope @pajones3
Twitter @pajones3
Instagram@pajones14

The Authors Speak
From Debra

Hidden Gems, a co-authored book, and workbook with my big sister, PJ and myself is a testament to God's amazing vision and purpose for our lives.

When this book started out, I did not intend for it to be a book at all! It was simply an observation of events that led us to look at what God was revealing through a simple, everyday event.

Often we expect God to do things in ways that that shoot off rockets and are very dramatic. However, we serve a God who has a still small voice. In that small voice, if we are quiet enough we can hear what He is saying and see how to bring His purpose to fruition. It just so happened that the quiet ones, in this case, were my sister and I. I happened to hear what God was saying during my shopping event, and my sister saw the vision to write it down and publish a book. PJ has always been the writer in the family and a big encourager. She went as far as copywriting the book eight years before its publishing date because she knew that it was something that was important to share with others. Without her vision, Hidden Gems would not exist.

My hope and prayer is that you can see yourself as the beautiful gem God created and to recognize the value in being encouraged, supported and mentored by those that have a vision that will propel you to the purpose God has for your life!

DEBRA D JONES
AUTHOR

Connect with Debra D Jones
www.DebraDJones.com
Periscope @debradjones
Facebook @debradjones
Twitter @debradjones
Instagram @debradjones

Acknowledgments

Thank you God! We can do nothing without you. We are grateful that you gave us the assignment of exposing *Hidden Gems*.

A huge shout out to Alice M. Baker who provided *CZ – An Interlude* as the bridge from *Hidden Gems - The Book to Hidden Gems - The Workbook*. We appreciate you more than you may ever know!

To our siblings: Minister Vivian, Claude Jr., Ronald, Robert, Richard and Brenda, we LOVE YOU and celebrate all the hidden gems of you that God has and is revealing!

From PJ

Warm wishes to my beloved nieces and nephews beginning with my oldest niece Jolonda, the Laven ders, Joneses, Gipsons, Parkers, Terrells, Garretts, Butlers, Seranos, Johnsons, and Haley; Our cousins Leitners and Harris.

Jaye, thanks for the Spotify music which helped me heal.

I would be remiss if I did not give a special shout-out to my great-nephew, Sean for assisting me and escorting

The Authors Speak

my walker and I from the Rehab to doctor appointments for months often with his baby in his arm.

Immense thanks to my daughter, Sonya, and son-in-law, Kwame for their assistance and support.

Thanks to Marquita and Hawa, my CNA's, Jessica, Monica and Mike my Physical and Occupational Therapists at the Clare Rehab.

Hugs for my Out-Patient Physical Therapist, Jason Kwat whose skills and abilities enabled me to walk again.

Last, but not least are my life-long friends, Ernestine, Sandra K, Leavon, their families and a host of other friends gained over the years.

About The Authors

Patricia 'PJ' Jones is an avid reader with a passion for short story writing since childhood. For many years she enjoyed interacting with and assisting people at a premiere Chicago hospital. PJ is ecstatic about her return to writing full-time. Scriptures included within Hidden Gems by her sister Debra also serve the purpose of interacting with and assisting people.

Debra D Jones is a corporate trainer and Minister of the Gospel. She was excited about the opportunity to collaborate with her big sister and fulfill their desire to see Hidden Gems in print. She is grateful to be part of a big, beautiful, loving family of gems.

www.ingramcontent.com/pod-product-compliance
Lightning Source LLC
Chambersburg PA
CBHW070938160426
43193CB00011B/1731